Mr. Paws Invents

by Aubrey Brown
illustrated by Marilyn Janovitz

Core Decodable 103

McGraw Hill Education

Bothell, WA • Chicago, IL • Columbus, OH • New York, NY

MHEonline.com

Send all inquiries to:
McGraw-Hill Education
8787 Orion Place
Columbus, OH 43240-4027

ISBN: 978-0-02-138980-3
MHID: 0-02-138980-2

Printed in China

10 11 12 13 14 DSS 29 28 27 26 25

"I invented this. It unscrews caps. It makes caps easy to open," Mr. Paws said.

"I dislike saying it, but this will not go well," Tom whispered.

Just then, bottles fell all over! Tom unplugged a red wire.

Mr. Paws said, "I invented this. It wraps and unwraps gifts."

"I disagree," Tom whispered. "It cannot wrap gifts and it cannot unwrap gifts! It can just smash gifts."

Tom had to disconnect green wires. He had to untwist black wires.

Mr. Paws did not see the mess.

"This opens locks. It can unlock this gate," Mr. Paws explained.

"That is untrue! It jams locks!" whispered Tom.
Tom had to yank the nails to get out.

Mr. Paws was in a yard. "This unwinds a hose. It unwinds a hose fast," he said.

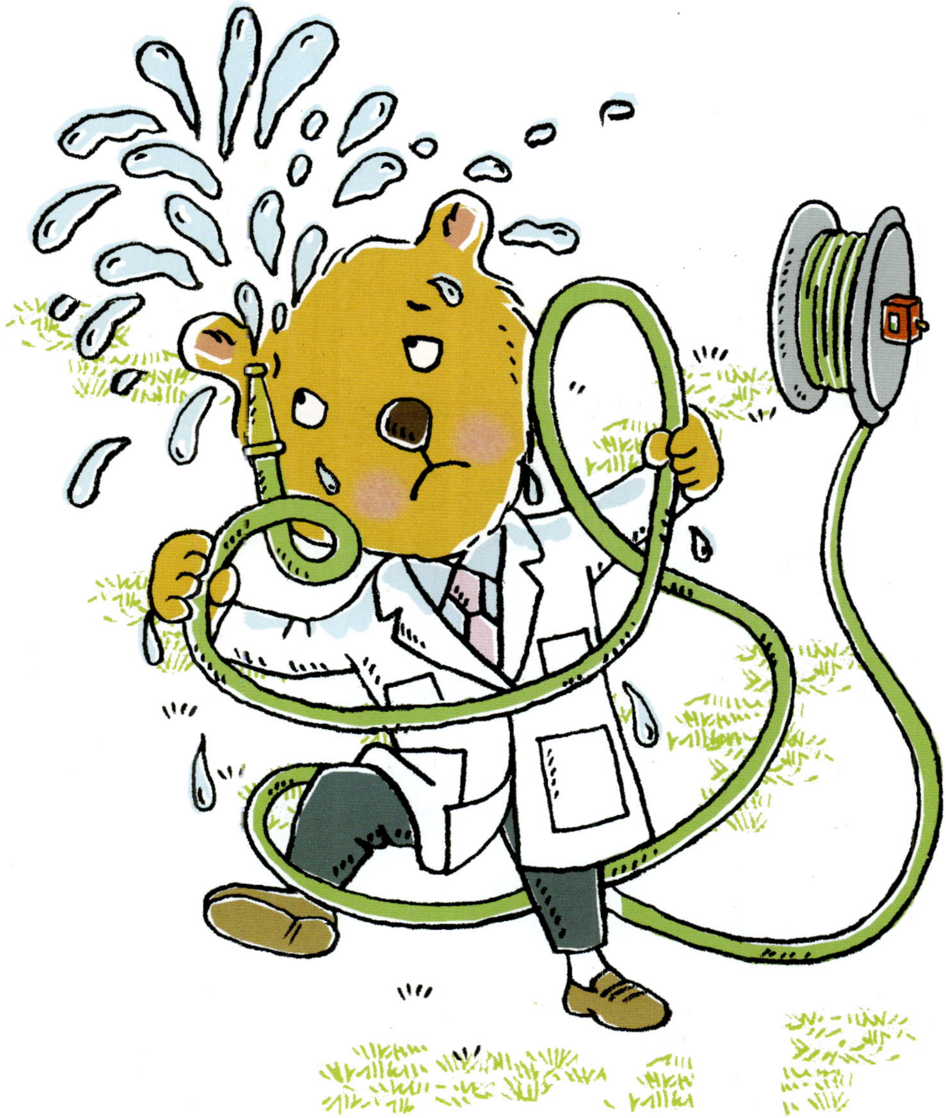

"It will not unwind the hose. It will make a knot!" whispered sad Tom.

He had to untie the hose.

Mr. Paws went back in the lab. "Is your bed unmade? This can make it!" he said.

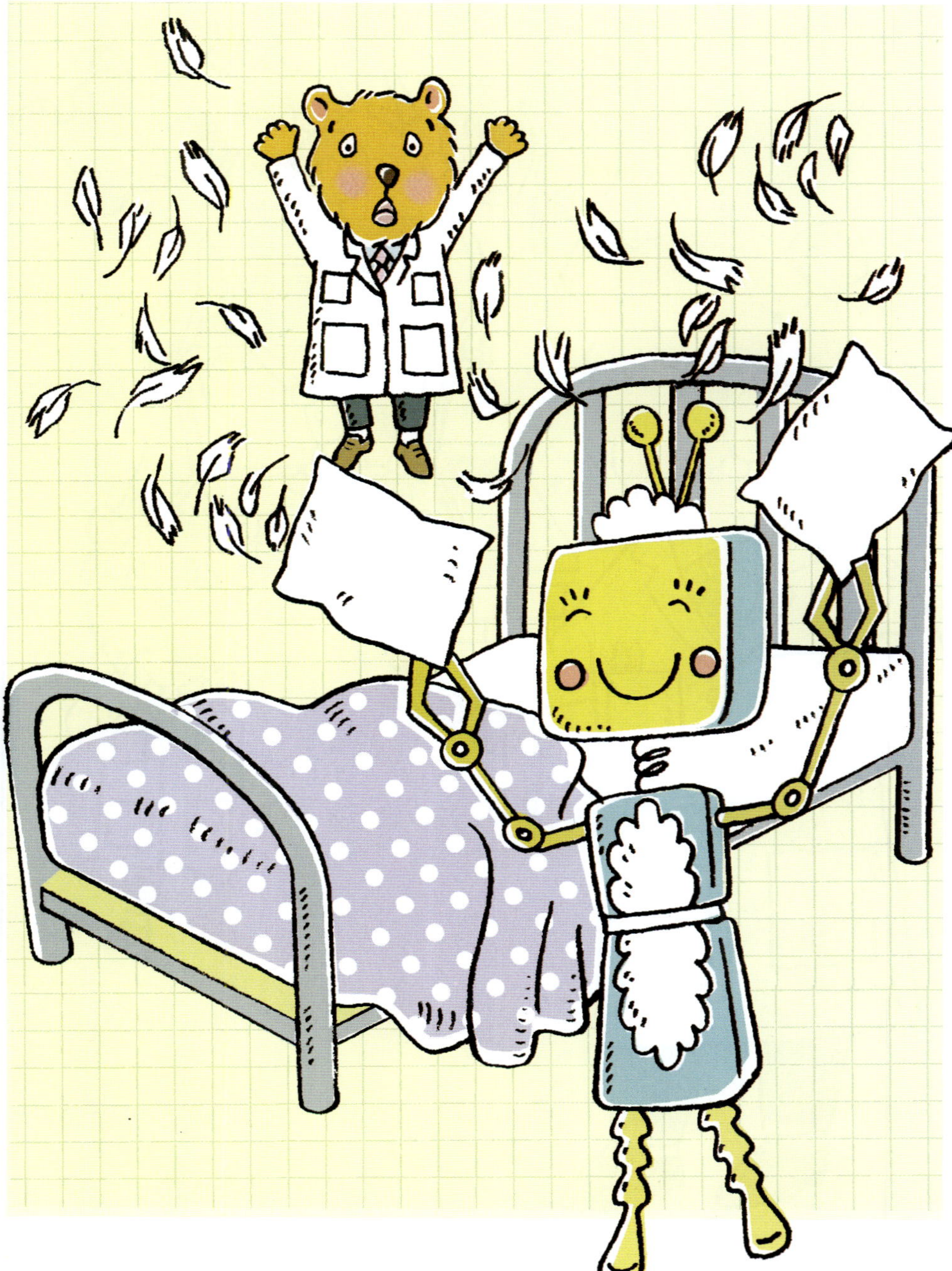

"No! It unmakes your bed. It shreds your mattress. It unstuffs your pillows!" Tom whispered.

"This unzips and unpacks a bag," said Mr. Paws.

"It rips the bag. It rips shirts and pants!" whispered Tom.

"This is Tom. If he did not help me, I would be unable to make things," said Mr. Paws.

Tom looked unhappy. "These things will get better," he whispered. Then he had to unplug more wires.